How Long She'll Last in This World

Camino del Sol

A Latina and Latino Literary Series

How Long She'll Last in This World

María Meléndez

THE UNIVERSITY OF ARIZONA PRESS

Tucson

The University of Arizona Press
© 2006 by María Meléndez
All rights reserved
Manufactured in the United States of America

11 10 09 08 07 06   6 5 4 3 2 1

Library of Congress Cataloging-in-Publication Data

Meléndez, María (María Teresa)
    How long she'll last in this world / María Meléndez.
       p. cm. – (Camino del sol)
    Includes bibliographical references.
    ISBN-13: 978-0-8165-2515-7 (pbk. : acid-free paper)
    ISBN-10: 0-8165-2515-3 (pbk. : acid-free paper)
    1. Hispanic American women—Poetry. 2. Nature—Poetry. I. Title.
II. Series.
PS3613.E446H69 2006
811'.6—dc22
                                                    2005017354

Publication of this book is made possible in part by the proceeds of a permanent
endowment created with the assistance of a Challenge Grant from the National
Endowment for the Humanities, a federal agency.

For John

CONTENTS

IV.

I.

Remedio

Let go your keys, let go your gun,
let go your good pen and your rings,
let your wolf mask go
and kiss goodbye
your goddess figurine.

There is a time to grip
your talismans,

a time to strip yourself of them.

Spirit and flesh
will have sometimes had enough

of go-betweens—

A refastening
of our noses and our ears

onto our soul

can only be accomplished
in the company of master exemplars.

Take wolves, each with a soul full of scents:

asperine willow leaves
and damp earth, willow-rooted.

At the end of summer, a wolf's soul hears

cottonwood catkins'
long trajectory down an ageless azimuth,

feels, in her inner ear,

myriad shifts of air
    as the tufty seeds ride twilit rays
        and glow as we imagine all
            eternal things to glow.

A remedy for when you've lost your sense
of Spirit in the world,

a simple spell for home lycanthropy:

    Smell the new season,
    acrid, tensed to grow
    in budding wolf willow,
    and feel the heat recede
    from a moose's corpse—then
    recuerda esta loba.

Recuerda . . . from the Spanish *recordar*
which is at root not remember or re-mind,

but pass back through the heart—

    let her pass back through your heart again,
    this wolf.

Backcountry, Emigrant Gap

I thought we fell asleep
austere and isolated—

two frogs calling across Rock Lake.

By morning, deer prints
new-pressed
      in the black ground between our tents—

      more lives move beside us
      than we know.

Why Not Attempt the Summit

Mount Shasta City, 1999

All night the buried mouths
    beneath our condos lecture us,
      we can hear their blather
    extrude up into the fir trees,
the diminishing clinks of words
    chiming minor keys
      on their way to the stars.
    Love as much as you
can, don't throw your heart
    away to just one god, wash
      the baby in mint, watch
    where you step on the mountain,
things that live so high
    don't want visitors.
      Feed them whiskey, concrete,
    cigarette or bone ash, doesn't matter,
nothing keeps them shut.
    So we trust their advice and vow,
      with our red and recycled breath,
    never to scramble or crawl above
the porous wall of trees
    that mark a crooked timberline
      along the gravel and scree.
    We'll only go far as the limber pines,
and won't presume to chase spirits
    over tinkling shales.
      We mind this limbed boundary
    because the town mechanic

crossed over it in a vision
    that almost killed him; andesite grains
        winked up at him from the highest slopes,
    and he drove into their dark fission
of mineral and glass;
    but when the valley drew his stone limbs down,
        the gravitational tow
    of his hoard of sleeping relatives
nearly tore apart
    his breath from bones, from heart;
        he tumbled out of the dream
    in a surge of scalding rock and scarlet vapors.
We don't tempt this verge
    because andesite is not a visionary's word,
        snow-wet andesite is
    metamorphic and too visionary,
and the tiny pink blooms
    of alpine Campanula (which deeply
        thinks to grow an inch
    each quarter century) would snare us
into slow, endless worship—
    our children would go hungry.
        (We know these perennials
    from stories that the dirt dreams up—)
We keep to our side of the trees
    because the firs themselves are near enough
        to provide sufficient comfort
    to subsist on, and so much
has already sloughed
    from the sure face of the land for us,
        and to learn the grace
    in songs to praise the spiders
living that high, we'd have to die
    or want to die and ever after hope

for nothing else but death.
        Because the need to be self-referential
every instant above treeline
        is lethally disorienting to us:
                always having to look at one's
        trunk to be assured of one's existence,
to look at oneself and not one's surroundings
        to verify what one is.
                In the alpine, only the winged
        know who they are in reference
to shifting slopes; we're not shaped
        to rise and flow on updrafts.
                We live behind the scar
        of this limit because there are no houses,
of devotion or otherwise, above
        the timber; because we were created
                in the firs' image and remain,
        like the firs, unclassifiable;
we try to prefer
        forest enclosure to Krumholz exposure
                because we need to ask for nothing
        from at least one space because great powers,
wild and hunted,
        sought and supplicated to,
                need a place to be left to themselves,
        to their own devices.
Pleading erodes creators
        under any circumstance,
                and there are no perfect worshipers
        for these gods outside all measures of perfection.
They need a high, storm-cleansed
        refuge, sparkling with silence,
                to perch and preen on when valley air
        becomes polluted by exhausted ghosts.

An Argument for the Brilliance of All Things

On a downed spruce at Murie Ranch,
branches curve like scoured whale ribs,
moss adheres as seaweed would.

An old ruffed grouse struts through the windfall,
drumming, drumming
its courtship ritual.

Yet still we hear the claim "human consciousness
consummates," as though matter waits, barren,
for its better half.

Meanwhile, grouse sperm
have every confidence
in the messy interlock

of matter with matter.
If, indeed, consciousness could be
extracted from the mountains

like iron ore, isolated
from shale beds—as crude—siphoned out
from the center of cells

like messenger RNA, could be
examined on a slide plate,
ex situ,

we'd have to admit
that its saline content
matches that of the ocean, a tear,

a teaspoon of semen, a ferning
droplet of amnion waters.
Know this, all humanists:

under the pure, lifeless
surface of the Sea
of Thought swims a great

gray whale, scarred
and barnacled, carrying
a calf, a great gray whale

about to breach.

Visitation

God save the amateurs

and their faith that something gorgeous
as a comet tumbles toward us
from outside the tidy orbit
we have known;

that some white-hot, divine refrain,
like an arpeggio of epochs,
will reverberate across
our fertile nights.

When a four-billion-year-old traveler
dazzled up the deep-sky mess
scanned and scoped (for simple joy)
by Bopp & Hale,

something must have started smiling
as it felt them both projecting
and attracting jagged bolts
of lightning hope.

When I moaned through my night labor,
its bright head and salty tail
beaded a blessing on my forehead,
and I pushed,

straining to show another shocker
through the cold hospital window,
and the glass fogged up with breath
on either side.

After the mash and sear of pain,
labia swollen to the size
of some magnificently bruised
magenta fruit,

with a small, burst vein streaking red
across my eye, time spread, open and warm
for the release
of this one smooth skein.

But the thirty-four-hundred years
between our species and the comet now
are dripping down like icicles
at noon;

yes, I should look to my son,
inhale the amber from his scalp,
but he, alone, is too small
to protect or redirect the coming flood

of generations. And the icy question
circles: Who will remain, what survives
Surprise's random
orbit?

In the Early Months of Snowmelt, 1997

In a cabin on the upper Ditch Creek drainage
of the Jackson Hole basin in Wyoming,

thick weekly paper, laid out tabloid-style,
brought word of a mudslide in Hoback Canyon

and a roundup of Mexicans, over one hundred of them,
hauled out of town in windowless, silver trailers.

Meanwhile, the elk were offered refuge on the valley floor,
in meadows near the hospital where I'd recently labored

to add one-quarter of a Mexican to the population
and discovered my life to be profoundly mammalian.

What could I say about the trailers? The dirty business
of keeping a limited class at leisure in mountain resorts?

Besides the newborn, I carried new depression around,
sorrow near to me as cord blood, disguised as one of life's

essential fluids. In my teens, I'd hiked the Tetons, practicing
the work that scientists do—describing the moss campion

and the class-3 ram, slogging through mud to revegetate
old horse camps. But I was utterly unschooled in the foolish

dialects of heart required to answer another whose needs
had latched completely onto mine. There is no field camp

for breastfeeders in training. *Walking on walking, underfoot*
earth turns—streams and mountains never stay the same.

Trudging with baby around our orbital on the campus
of Teton Science School (cabin to dining lodge, work in the office,

dining lodge, cabin), I lugged a diaper bag stuffed tight as a
summit pack: two burp cloths, extra onesies, changes of clothes,

at least six diapers (Huggies velcro when we could afford them),
box full of wet wipes, fleece bodysuit, hat and mittens, plastic

bags for leaked-on clothes, pacifier, thin swaddling blankets,
thick playtime blanket to spread on wood floors, chew toys, changing pad,

nursing pads, diaper cream. A neighbor, young woman, sneered at me
as she sauntered out to an evening ski, "Is all that really necessary?"

On a rare walk alone to Upper Meadow, I tried to identify
the green shoots growing up between the bones

of an old moose cow, winterkill from years ago,
her stout skeleton still guarding the remains

of an unborn calf. Trips to town were my more
typical adventure: Teton Valley Books and the County Library,

housed in an old log building on King Street. I checked out
books on Big Things to keep me company as I cared for a tiny

person in my one-room home with my one body,
torn and swollen. Sometimes I'd read out loud,

sitting on the bed with the small boy propped in the bend
of my knee, blinking up at me, stories and poems

come to us by way of a Colombian, a Wyoman, and a mountaineer
of the mind. The titles may be familiar to any woman or man

who's ever tried to rise from the billowy weight
of a long winter: *One Hundred Years of Solitude, Resurrection Update,*
                            Mountains and Rivers Without End.

Buckrail

1.   —rise, strong as a buffalo, from the slumping body
tied eighteen hours to a buckrail fence—

All your life, you had known this fence.
X-and-crosspole pattern, wood left rough—
This is the West, where men are men and beauty
sweeps down from the sky in a cold wind
that batters any color face raw and pink.

Handgun smashed against your skull
over and over, only sagebrush
met your eye; frost-spiked air
for your mind to grab hold of and rise—

2. I've never been attacked
by a bull bison, but I lived
beside one in a Wyoming winter.
He walked past my cabin each dusk,
bellowing like a lion scrawling
territory lines of sound
across the landscape.

That same winter, up north in Yellowstone,
rangers shot eleven hundred bison
as they plodded down a plowed road
out of the park, noses tuned to the pitch
of grass-scent further west.
(Killed them to save cattle
from a rumor of contagious
bison disease.)

Four times this old bull
pawed his way into my dreams
             (bluff-charged once, spoke once:
             I need your babies for a carpet,
             once stood in profile with an inverted crown
             of gold-brown hairs tufted out between his legs;
             once stationed two front hooves and giant face
             inside my doorway), proving
he could occur naturally
anywhere in this land.

3.   Every nine seconds in America
hate   a star is knocked loose
and begins to burn down the sky
until the speed of falling
buries its light   *crime*

4. I missed the chance to sing for you,
left the Rockies' front range two years before
a volatile wick would ignite between two boys
who would see you playing pool and want you
snuffed out. Queerest thing about it all was
Rainbow Chorus singing for the newscast vigil
the night after your murder.
I'd sung second soprano with them
and knew all the words to the melody
underscoring the reporter's solemn face.

> *When you need a light*
> *in the lonely night, carry me*
> *like a fire in your heart. . . .*

I'd joined as a "straight but not narrow"
protester against Amendment 2,
and narrowly missed realizing the weight
of the chorus' mission: not swatting
at laws, but cementing together
a bulwark of music against the slaughter of boys.

5.   The kid who finally found the body
fell off a mountain bike along the fencerow,
told police that, at first glance,
he "thought it was a scarecrow."
                              Matthew,
I've loved the range you were born into,
and there's something that kid wasn't telling:
before he saw your swollen face, your blue hands tied
like calves' feet, when he first looked up, a massive bull-bison
fixed its silver eyes on him and roared.

6.   You keep singing, *This is home,*
                       I don't belong
                                  anyplace else. Matthew
              Shepard, carry us now
              through the haze of our frozen breath,
              through this drifting, chest-deep fear.

Aullido

In the Sierra Madre
    they say, "El alma de
un lobo nunca desaparecía
    de este mundo"—

a wolf's spirit never
    disappears from the forest.
"Siempre su espíritu
    estaba pendiente de vigilar

todo lo que había
    a su alrededor;
era el protector
    de los bosques."

Can you picture a wolf's spirit?
    It's not the gray, wispy thing
screen-printed as background
    on countless tees.

It's solid as granite,
    forged in fire, firm
as the basement rock
    of the Rocky Mountains.

Can you picture a wolf's
    spirit as sculptor
of the moose, the cottonwoods,
    even the willows?

It is mammalian and familial:
  there is a loba spirit flowing
in your breast milk and in the milk
  of elk, moose, deer.

So come back here, loba,
  recuerda estas montañas, mother mountains:

  San Juan Range, Sierra del Huacha, Culebra Range, Spanish Peaks,
  Front Range, Snowy Range, Sierra de la Encantada, Sawatch Range,
  Gore Range, White Mountains, Black Range, Mogollon Mountains,
  Burro Mountains, Sierra del Nido, Sierra Madre.

Living wolf, spirit in flesh,
  breathe here,
walk here, recall these places
  you never left.

Glance again in time's long mirror
and recognize yourself.

II.

In Biruté's Camp

Suppose God is looking for a good
      piece, who could be you with that bare
          strip of scalp parting your long hair,
    braided loose and looped up in the swamp heat,
sweat curling around your small, bristly eyebrows,
      your hands gleaming with juice and pulp
          as you hammer fruit on the feeding platform.

     That strange orangutan,
the human-raised one called Pan-gan,
      who throws men off the dock
          like an overzealous baptizer, may
    be a god and here he comes
          padding side to side onto your platform in the swamp.
    If he curves the ridiculous length of his
tendon-riddled arms around your waist
and wrestles you down to the wooden boards,
   scream—he'sbitingyouhe'stryingtokillyou—no,
he's pushing up your skirt—

      become limp below the waist and make your torso
  a flexible branch for him to squeeze
      as he swivels from one world to the next;
    (now he is calm and deliberate,

                  now his eyes roll upward)—

    When he finally moves off
      the feeding platform and into the trees,
         rise into this loss, which is relief:
  his seed will shimmer out of you, unrecognized.

Art of Combat

For the amateur fighters at Capitol Boxing Gym, Sacramento, CA

Ponytail out the back of her headgear,

        she punches air,

swings at the mirror, prepares

        for eye contact in the ring.

Her own eyes now are not her own,

        they stand in for the opponent.

Me, I could never punch a girl.

        But I might like a girl to hit me

so I could feel the power in a female fist.
(pray with me now)
        Oh, split my lip!

But she steps in there alone,

        leans on the ropes,

shoulders back, arms falling slack

        like water off of stone;

checkin' the scene like a king

        surveying funked-out hinterlands,

hands just beginning to sweat

        in her red leather gloves.

Learning to Speak: Carolina

After we emptied the Mayflower truck,
boxes torn open, piles of rumpled baby
pajamas, wrinkled skirts and

    Night: a black cloth soaked in song,

a lime-green animal
rested its long, six-legged body
high on a bare white wall.
Katydid.

    Soil ("soul"): doe-brown sand.

Some days here, blood lands
in the yard: Cardinal.
None of us are ever safe—

a scorpion in the crib, for example.

    Winter: Kalmia blooming,
    eight stamens bent back like leg-hold traps—

    Too much unnamed space
on the sharp map, too much unimplied life
dangling from the black ink web
of new expressways.

    Coast: where a year hissed and rolled at our ankles.

    Salt Marsh: honey-reek of cordgrass
    and a local chuckling, giant pocket watch
    (Crabpot) hung over the dock—

And the baby, as always, experiments:
pushes around a small red bus
with circles inside for round little people.
He wedges a chubby foot in the window,
filling two empty rows—

>Longleaf Pine: *the brother who stayed,*
>*he holds the light of stars.*

he learns to put his foot
in his own little sandal. By next month,
his foot will have grown—

One or more of the terms is always changing;

don't tell him
the world will accommodate any shape,
will make a place for him,
will hold him or bite him or touch him
as he pleases, caress him like rain,
no matter his vastness—

>Pleiades: *the boys who left us.*

A Different Sympathy

If the cord snared
your raw vagina when you pulled
your purple newborn up
to nurse, and every suck was cat-
tongue, nipple smashed, demanding
milk you couldn't make yet
and no one told you, "It's all right,
you will become numb as polished stones,
flow with life," then two days later,
veins in your breasts turned hot-iron hard,
and the magmatic flood of your milk
drenched all your clothes, stank up your room,
stained your bed, and no one told you,
"It's all right, this roar of pain
will soon recede into a trickle,"

and if, on a slow walk,

you saw the river's bulging edge,
where waters gouge troughs
with loyal licking,
where a cow moose's tracks
yield up in grainy swirls
and dissolve,
then you, too, would hunt for reeds,
weave a tiny boat; humming low
old songs, you'd push your son
to root on the breast
of the river.

Arborphilia Pantoum

The shock of seeing you standing alone
    (in the brittle grasses) manzanita,
        reaches of red bark thin and smooth as throat skin—
the closer I walk, the more your color divides,
    manzanita in brittle grass;
        (touching you feels like touching my baby son)
the closer I walk, the more deep red dissolves
        into orange, black, and yellow, streaming through,
        like touching the skin of my baby son
    when we can't get enough of each other
    (yellow, black, orange, getting enough of you);
        he'll squeeze my breasts in the bath, shriek, "Mama!,"
when we can't get enough of each other—
he'll grab my face with butterfly hands,
    poke for the corner of my eye, "Mama eyes!,"
        as I rub soap on his round little tummy;
he'll grin, hold my face in butterfly hands,
        grope with his feet for the slope of my belly
        as I hold him, rub soap on his round little tummy.
Who is it I'm stroking, my hand on this branch,
    remembering feet on the slope of my belly
        as your red arms grope the paths of my brain;
who is it I'm stroking, my hand on this branch,
    and what will my fingers have taught you,
        with your red arms forking into my brain—

the spark of desire arcs out of my palms, into your veins,
and will my fingers at least have taught you
the seeping oil of my skin, rooted child—
the spark of desire arcs out of my palms, into your veins,
reaches of red bark thin and smooth as throat skin;
loneliness oils my bones, rooted child,
at the shock of seeing you standing alone.

Nude Sonnet

When studied apart from chickadees and crooked paths, you seem built of
                                                                    concave lines
        (scoop of shoulder blades, curving pectoral base,
        crescent canoe of pubic hair hung from pelvic bones,
        soft swoop of glutes, furrowed muscles along the spine);
I'm guilty of examining your form uncomplimented, unembraced—
sink-fixing, baby-washing, goddamn hockey-watching man,
tolerant, tolerant man, why don't you ever say I'm beautiful, but then,
why don't I ever say that you are? I'm checking skin at the boniest place
of your ankle, and even there it's smooth; consulting the stubborn
worry lines bowed across your forehead, divining the asterisk of hair,
*size of a silver dollar (cupped between your collar bones), querying the air
along the part (can you believe it) in your armpit to learn if you were born
on the same stained sheets that I was; but any guilt you bear is sown
in hairs sprouting like a trail of needle grass to your navel: beautiful man,
                                                unscoutable meander, my own.

Good News for Humans

Destruction hasn't been your only story.
All living things beyond you that you've loved,
you've made love live in them: at the junction
of chocolate & cream-colored rings on the king
snake's skin, in the morning sparkle of cows'
dewy slobber all over the pasture, in the powerful
slice of a gator's tail, in the 5 a.m. ruckus
of a capercaillie lek (males squawk and spin, even when
no female's near), in the scraggly herd
of tule elk stepping through patchy fog
in the green coast hills; you've made love
live on the tops of hippos' ever-growing
teeth, and in the osprey's perfect talon-open moment
before splashdown, in the monkey's
soft hair, and in the four toes
on a gray wolf's hidden print; just by noticing
the sparkling blue gem at the dragon's forehead,
you've made love live there, too.

You've placed love on this earth gently as a mother
gorilla puts a baby to her breast.
Thanks to the Academy of Mommies,
especially the Indian elephant ladies
and the lactating grizzlies, you've meted out a fierce,
nutrient love, and it's regal as the guttural purr
of a sleepy lion.

You've even jammed a ladybug-sized love
between the *Homo* and the *sapiens,*

meaning love now walks the streets
at all hours.

Thanks to the cinnamon-colored black bear,
you've made a love that flares
beyond categories, love with the snarly strength
of a badger's nose, daring as the gray fox
raising kits under the shed.

You've let love steal
into camp, eat scraps
and piss on leather boots, marmot-style,
and you've let it loose
to twirl and leap in the calls of *Grus
canadensis*. Your love's elastic
as the arms of a praying mantis, and it feeds
backyard suet to the greedy
pine siskin, too tiny
to ever blow anything up. If you can
love a sociopathic cat named Doctor Jesus,
or a tarantula writhing through a secret molt,
you can expect some loving looks
from their creator.

You've sprouted dusty crow wings by this love
that lets you fly to the top of a telephone pole
and perch easy next to the greasy
she-crow with the huge, voluptuous
brain.

Thanks to you, love has the highest view
on top a giraffe's four long
miracles. You've made love undulate,
jungular and oceanic, in tiger
and dolphin music, and you've brought love into the nest

of the mountain bluebird. Amor in you,
amor outside of you has been
the old bluetick hound's end-of-driveway howl,
and the growl, too, of the alpha male wolf
under serious threat.

The little loaded springs of love
in your every cell, well, they exploded
and made the fuzzy head and dirty
feet of a little boy:
joy in red overalls, inventing new ways to defeat
gravity, and out of a whole planet worthy
of your dreams, thankfully you've remembered to love especially
the duck-billed platypus.
Thank beastliness!—this love that's made us
claw-hearty, beak-sturdy
enough for life.

III.

Collections of Nearly Unlovable Spaces

In this arboretum I've got Bare Ground Sickness, understory withdrawal.
The thing that writes itself here could be fire, burning the pattern of a catamount
                                                                    print.

No interpretive signage says, "Chinese Railroad Worker was hung from this Live
                                                                    Oak."
Places and pasts are simultaneous places and times in the open mind.

A cluster of us won't leave the hills, fog, bored mule deer, and prefab homes.
I blame the addictive water we drank as kids, laced with traces of quicksilver.

Phases of the madrone tilting into cold nights. Hard green berries begin to blush.
String them up from Memory's throat, her breath a vanilla drench of evening
                                                                    blossoms.

What we are (a boy) practicing (was hanged) is suffering (here),
which everybody practices, but strangely few grow graceful in.

Kids throwing rocks at ducklings. Kids pitching stones between ducks.
White shank of egret neck against green water.

Wells, pipes, wires get "shrubbed up"—architect's slang for hidden.
Codes for not resisting red penstemon blooms got shrubbed up in the hands of
                                                                    my son.

Tule fog, no guarantees on middle distance; animals bounce echoes off each
                                                                    other's hides.
Over there, the well-motor grinding, or scrub jays shrieking like acorn-mad
                                                                    preachers.

Sinking fog, please spread the Gap(s) of Putahtoi. A mall is the new river fork.
(Even in Putahtoi,
     tule fog damp in my hair,
         I long for Putahtoi.)

Tonacacihuatl: Lady of Our Flesh

Sacramento Valley

Fragrance of the rain in her breath. The dampness
at the back of her knees smells like rain also.
She appears with a shining crow the color of cinnabar,
and a mark at her shoulder blades displays the same crow.

Poison has made her throat lovely. For that poison,
praise is chanted in heat-meters making triple-digit noise.
Part of her has the form of a tule stem, and that form
she can absorb, if she wants it hidden. And it is hidden!

How many spirits she's twin to, and how long she'll last in this world,
are secrets stashed in the rattle
of corn ears, in the coils
of venomous snakes.

Thirteen mirrors spangle her dress. For those sun-round mirrors,
praises are chanted by thirteen thousand red-legged hoppers.
At noon, she steps out of a culvert and collides with the naked light,
and her fever is an affliction known as August.

So she is, Lady of Our Flesh, who is what is.
Is she not here, who is our mother?
Huffing, with matted hair, she stamps a shovel blade
to begin a small grave.

Controlled Burn

23 April '99 (one month before we burn the prairie):

1030, wind: N, 35mph

We don't know exactly when the first burn day will be. Everything depends on the weather. The Fire Marshall gave us a six-week window, but the Air Quality Board has to approve burns on a day-by-day basis. For maximum safety, winds can't exceed 15mph.

> No one is bombing Jepson Prairie—
> young wheatgrass whips forward
> like green taffeta unrolled and shaken—
> Low overhead, a fuel carrier pointing east,
> gray Air Force whale floating in the sky.
> The grasses look natural.
> The delta green ground beetle survives
> nowhere else in the world—
> The plane seems not to move.

July '98: Pre-burn grass survey:

Bethany lifts her khaki tank top in the heat to let the wind across her belly. We're on Jepson Prairie Reserve, where no one knows what gives the land its small mounds and hummocks. Maybe, as it is the nature of water to meander, so it is the nature of soil to vary its surface.

> I murmur grasses' names
>   *(Nasella pulcra, Elymus glaucus)*
> as though they were retardants
>   for subsurface ardor.

The wide, shallow depression next to the road will fill with winter rain and become Olcott Lake, a large vernal pool. Life that sprouts in the lake changes shape as summer dries the water. Coyote thistles' floating leaves shrivel away, and they put down deep, strong roots. Fairy shrimp leave legions of eggs peppering the mud of the lake bed, where they'll wait for the next wet season. Shrimp eggs can live in the mud for a hundred years.

One week before we burn the prairie:

As Reserve Manager, Bethany is not afraid to exercise dissatisfaction with the land. We bounce along in her pickup toward the site of our first ignition, and she explains the reasons for burning. *Cleansing the prairie of invasive exotics, plants that don't belong. Insects around here need native flowers like blue lilies, goldfields, wild violets, and native bunchgrasses. The natives are adapted to fire, so a good burn will get rid of the nasty star thistle, wheatgrass, and this stuff,* she tilts a bristly grass spike between her fingers, *this medusa head is the really bad stuff.* Would she feel differently if that grass were named "prairie arrow"?

Her hair must smell like violets

all spring long.

The night before we burn the prairie:

How can I say what is this place and what isn't? Maybe the mountains are a temporary spasm of the prairie and what's beyond them is also the prairie.

Forget buried eggs and conservation. There are half-collapsed bridges in the Balkan countryside, and Beth, I want to spoon daylight into your thin, dry mouth.

The lake raises its hackles.

Fairy shrimp swim upside down—

a thousand hidden lights.

Two weeks before we burn the prairie:

Bethany believes in moral imperative and therefore supports the bombing. She says, "In this world, we have to look out for each other." I can't argue.

———

Also on the prairie: Kinsmen Go Kart Club, Travis Air Force Base, power lines. To judge a piece of land, ask what it is providing, and to whom.

Courage alone will not suffice. Nor will any amount of facts. What was the speed of that last wind gust? Do goldfields make her sneeze? Who's actually dying?

> Brown tint of annual grasses dying off already.
> The first black gnats crawl under my hat.
> Everything is relevant to the obsessed.

In the month before we burn the prairie:

From a friend in Greece: "When I hear that cloud cover kept NATO from bombing as much as it wanted, or that clear skies allowed the bombing to be increased, I look out my window—the weather they're talking about is my weather, too."

Love interrupts, the land interrupts, all history is natural.

One week before we burn the prairie:

The message beneath Bethany's restoration vision is, "Don't get too attached to what's here. This is not what this place should look like." But it's too late, I already love what I see—

> All her visible surfaces
> are shades of a caramel spectrum.
> I know the value
> of the sugary skin that rounds the inner mound
> of her thumb-muscle,
> the significance of tan on the smooth backs
> of her hands.

Three days before we burn the prairie:

NATO jets returning from sorties jettison their undelivered bombs in the Adriatic Sea. The Italian government has not been informed.

The fairy shrimp lays eggs every day,
 trailing them behind her in a billowing sack.
I can see through her body.
 She is already bursting.

Alberto Pescadore, Adriatic harvester for twenty years, loops a rope around his
hand—hauls in enormous, lethal roe.

The day before we burn the prairie:

How can I say the eucalyptus trees around my townhouse are not Bethany?
Wind ignites their gentle clatter, "We fit into this dirt—"

———————

 How many species of grass are out here?
 Over 70.
 But how many, exactly?

———————

War smolders beneath the media term "crisis" and can be inserted anywhere.
For example:

 [   ] has daily offspring, [   ] doesn't know, exactly, how many,
 [   ] can live in the mud for a hundred years.

The first day we burn the prairie:

We were ready to burn Monday, but the wind kept gusting up to twenty.
We were ready Tuesday, but the water pump on the back of Virgil's flatbed
wouldn't start. Today, the wind is barely up to eight, the pump works, eleven
folks are suited up in flame-retardant Nomex suits with eleven bright yellow
helmets, two hoses, three backpack sprayers, four flappers, a truck with sodas
and donuts, a drip torch, and a green light from the Air Quality Board; *we're
ready,* as one ecology intern says, *to light this bitch.* Bethany closes the yellow
drape over her nose and mouth and lights a twenty-foot-wide line against the
prevailing wind. Two men lay down wetline on either side of the slow-burn-
ing fire. The rest of us roam the growing black swath to put out glowing sheep
dung. Everyone wants to watch the flames, but Bethany reminds us all to

watch downwind for spotfires. The safety of neighboring ranches depends on
how alert we can be to unplanned "blow ups."

> I have to fight
>> the urge to watch her
>>> boots plunging with every wind shift
>> into smoke.

The third day of burning:

I'm promoted to secondary hose, lay a jagged wetline that I learn to even out
as morning passes. Wind shift, blaze blows suddenly toward us. No one says,
"Put it out!" so I try to keep my line ahead of the flames, trotting backwards,
stumbling over the hose. Our frenzy hypnotizes us: wet the tall grass, here
she comes, wet the tall grass, here she comes. The hoses run out of water too
quickly, so it burns for twenty more minutes of frantic flapper and backpack-
shooter work.

After we finally kill the fire, I walk back over the blackline. Native saltgrass
spikes up with only leaf-tips singed. I kick the dark, feathery topsoil with the
toe of my boot; a thin spiral of smoke emerges. The humus is still smoldering
underground.

And in the papers:

> Peace could be
>> near, peace may be near,
> peace is near,
>> peace may be at hand.

Four days after we finish burning:

The black gnat bites that started out as little bumps are bright orange mounds,
almost slimy, like they want to ooze something. Most bites are under my ear
and just below the ribbing at the neck of my tee shirt. Season's over, odds are I
won't see Bethany again until next spring.

(But I'm always talking about you,
        I'm only talking
about you, your name
            means "home.")

All I didn't know before I knew this place—

        —that fairy shrimp abide most of their hidden lives
                in dimpled spheres, waiting to explode
                    in their own small sea;

        —what home, what peace, what anything could mean;

        —and the kiss of a drip torch on the earth,
                the blackness that they open out together.

American Adhaan

October 2001

Watch night spalling to the western edge
of invisible, its cool surrender
to the peach-colored breccia
of sunrise clouds (just water
                that has lately collapsed
                into form).

   How violently natural
my petroliferous valley looks
in this faint, blue wash;
the slow, arc'd strokes
of a great egret's wings
deny the crude thickness
of this air.

   The shattered world's particulates
fall everywhere around us;
the call to prayer means bowing
and facing them all.

An Illustrated Guide to Things Unseen

Here's the turquoise cheek
of a fathead minnow,
netted from the camo-tint
    can't-ever-see-what's-in-it creek;
   dropped on your palm, its glowing lilac thread
 of spine bisects your lifeline.

                Here's the spirit of a rhododendron garden
                  (slurp slurp slurp it's all for show)
                impersonating "Redwood Grove" in an arboretum.

      Here: two pipevine swallowtails,
          crazy with the indigo smell of each other,
   spiraling past a grinning red cat
      in the ivy, past a bearded man
         on a picnic bench who's leaving
            a short-haired woman, here's
               anger fastening over her
                  like an acorn cap.

Here's a rapist's habitat
between snowberry bushes
and live oak shadows.

              Here's a whole night
      heron rookery in a cottonwood,
    and here's a woman feeding stuffing
   to the ducks; she has bitten the tip
  of her baby's little finger.

Here, the reburied bones
of the First Woman exhumed during
construction of a Performing Arts center—

        Here's a poisonous oleander,
        concealing a well (and not so well,
                after all)
        from hypothetical polluter-terrorists.

For those of you suffering
from absence of riverflow,
    here's bowlegged Waterman
        stuck in the ground ("vacuum breaker");
  within his corroded metal,
      swish and rattle of water tumble,
        unlappable; its curling rhythm
      mimics the undercurrent of silence
    in the waterway you're trying to love,
      the unyielding laminar surface
      that's breaking your heart.

One-Minute Wail

(Just add Carbaryl!)

This valley never spawned a religion of emptiness, not with Early Girls
lining the causeway like lice from the backs of elephant trucks.

Put in sheep to barber the bushy tomatoes,
recover some losses after the plant has closed.

Kids always sympathetic to the wind, opening windows
on the school bus to let it in like a beggar.

I was born in the blurry mind of the desert in rain, came here to take my
place among rows of olive trees, old scholars lined up at a urinal.

(Who cares if words are emptiness, they motor things along
like a thin, strong muskrat tail.)

· (Who cares if they are tiny compared to the tendrilous galaxy?)

Heavy-lidded bucks watch out for us from between the branches.
Just as crushed buckeye powder stuns fish for harvest, so does crop dust
stun us; we float up on our backs to flat, blue heaven and wait for a meal.

Swerving through a storm of corn debris, I'd like to tip my head and drink up
all the yellow duster has to offer.

Recipe for When You're Tired of Feeding Your Family Life Cereal from a Box

bed of coals
fist-sized stones
strong fan
manzanita berries
understanding for the lives of yellow jackets
dry kindling
basket tray
boiling basket

Before light has tickled yellow jackets awake, build a fire close to their nest hole in the ground. Push smoke down the hole with the wide fan you wove last winter. After the yellow jackets are paralyzed by the smoke, dig out the nest. Carry it to a prepared bed of coals. Roast the nest. Shake out the dead larvae onto a basket tray. Mash them, then boil in a basket with hot stones. Drain and serve with manzanita berries.

The Seven Gates to Aztlán (for Mixedbloods)

Raza movement must be wrong, Aztlán can't be the Southwest,
too many giant cucarachas, there's no mention of pests
in accounts of the mythical homeland.
It could be aquí en California, except for the river
of Argentine ants on my counters, which I bait
with arsenic-laced appetizers, but in the middle of
wiping ants off the baby food jar, I realize
     defense of territory is an entrance to Aztlán.
       Crosshairs
         mark the target range
           across this tunnel of light.

What binds us more tightly to a place than eating and excreting?
They don't call it the food chain for nothing;
let's drink a mango smoothie, toss the islands back slick—
unless we choose not to have such a big mouth,
like Nabhan, in the Sonoran, who ate only
what grew within 100 miles of his home.
I hear he did this for a year, and I hear he recently moved.
     Eat, drink, and be wary in Aztlán!
       Silvery shapes (pondweed, crawdad, pondweed, heron)
         form and reform
           as they cross this mouth.

Dead crow under a cottonwood, clutching the twig
that broke beneath her in a windstorm, say, "That last flight's
real short, distance from a corvid's heart
to a human baby's pulse," say, "Cull the alkaline
emptiness from my sockets, boil it into an indigo slag,

take a dose and be whole again
in the eye of confusion."
    No secret death's a way into the mythical homeland.
            Cedar branches
                leach the rain
            that falls on this trapdoor.

Here in poetatlán, cuervotlán, fresatlán, osotlán,
place of poets, crows, berries, and California grizzlies,
it must be Aztlán, because the Aztatl (white herons we call egrets)
nest here, and they do not move to Oregon in search of scenic beauty.
Herons shock picky home-seekers by staying locked into their place,
-tlán being "place of" and "tooth," as in "rooted." I've seen Great Blues
raise twenty broods in a cottonwood next to a railroad
        ("Oigan hijos, it's more scared of you . . ."); so the spiraling descent
        that started somewhere else (across this bridge, that border, that gap)
        and ends up Here, the feathered glory in that white rush,
        is a gateway to Aztlán.
            Sky blue tunnel:
                fall through, fall through,
                the roof of this cave is on fire.

Go ask your local wise flowers, they'll tell you about the surge and curl
of landscape change. This is a long flower war, and the theater
between valley oaks is budding with goatgrass and star thistle, what's next?
It's a long flower war, and on the ground between sagebrush bushes,
cheatgrass has the present advantage, pero quién sabe?
Put the toloache to your ear, it drains sounds down
to the underground ear of Big Mind.
        At night, a thousand floral entrances unfurl—
            Cross-pollinate the worlds
                with moonlight as your guide;
                every scent that makes you tremble is your home.

As my teacher said, "We are nowhere, except, maybe, here,"
with millennia rolling past Targets and Borders and Gaps,
and the closer you look, the more it all seems
like a silky layer of water
on new-frozen ice, and this freaky set
of circumstances, this fake diamond
(strung from pure gold around our necks),
      "realidad," is an old cat-door into the mythical homeland.
                  Expensive ironwork
                     bars this entrance;
              rats sneak out and in.

Todos los viejos, and the parent rock of the Tehama formation,
they all have a place they came from before "before." By tracing origins
not just from a family tree, but from serpentine stones
and heron hatchlings, this doorway gets bigger. . . .
Night herons can't discriminate between their own broods
and those of their neighbors; they'll feed any
      open, nestling-shaped mouth. Enter anywhere the universe
      is becoming; feed anyone's babies en toda la gran familia.
                 This circle seems a moss-lined bed for eggs,
                    but like a black hole, it converts
                         bodies into shouting incandescence.

IV.

A Secret Between Lady Poets

How we two lust after news
          from the Peterson case,
wife & child pulled from the Bay,
          dripping wire & weeds & rec boat refuse—
talk of the Coffin Birth, coroner's slang
          for a dead child's delivery
from an already deceased mother; submerged
          as they were for months, we
picture all tissues softened and elegantly
          torn like damp newspaper,
baby's lips ragged and fluttering like some lilting
          anemone, both of them suffused
by the faint light found in lurid
          aquarium displays—it's a fact
your husband's just been stashed,
          ashy and silent, in the baby blue
urn on your piano. Too bad—he would've enjoyed
          the defendant's fish story:
"I wasn't boating in order to dispose of a body,
          I was trolling for sturgeon. With lures."
"Oh, sure!" Walt would've chuckled sarcastically,
          knowing that tackle's for bass or muskie.
Me, I'm here for the night, on leave
          from mothering and wifely duties,
making a mourning visit to you, teacher, friend,
          mother-in-tangled-language, because

we've got to keep an eye out together for whatever
                    the hell happens next. You've been breathing
under the water of grief, I've been sliding through the marsh
                    of my own maturation,
swaying between believing, unbelieving,
                    what was early beaten into me
about my built-in moral defect, naughty mollusk.
                    If ingesting the gore of the world with you
is a favor, it's the least I can do.
                    So we sip our Court T.V.
all night, eat green grapes so engorged
                    they're almost see-through.
Desperation and loneliness lap outside
                    your full, square house,
waves that rise to douse us with desire
                    for higher lunacy.
Up on the main floor, with God's
                    chilly wind in our faces
we can't be bothered with fear anymore,
                    we're gaining access
to the carving hand of the Holy,
                    we're slowly exploding
into nun-ness, and moonlight
                    slanting through the blinds
tracks right through us, translucent as mist
                    rising from the surface of sorrow.
We're sorceresses now, source and mouth, all delta,
                    pure, salty confluence
of the world's terrible, originary forces;
                    the remains of our lost lives
curdle and foam on the shore, display
                    the power of decay to begin

the parturition required
>to unfasten dead familial bonds.
We slip into the continuum
>of women destroyed or nearly destroyed,
women who surface in frightening forms
>and wreak their stories on shores.

Llorona's Guide to Baptism

Even though the museum in Berkeley's run off with the skull,
hide the mammoth's twelve-pound hunk of broken tusk
for yourself—after all, you discovered it.

As for the water: any creek
with fish storing enough mercury
to damage a human fetus
will do. Any waterway modern enough
to give you this recurring dream: Throw daughter in,
                                      then jump in after her.
                                      There she is, on top of a gravel bar,
                                      no crawdads hiding under her yet,
                                      no aquatic plants
                                      anchored to her belly. Pull her up,
                                      why   won't   she   focus   ?

(Cough and wheeze your way into each day.)

Wander the valley and wail for her plump forearms and wrists,
the safety of the fur she thinks she's grabbing in that fist,
hiss at the water she drinks every day,
you've already thrown her in.

Carry the tusk in your duffel,
say it's just a bunch of heavy books,
since you cannot smash the metallic creek
nor bash in your own head,
cannot holler through the ivory millennia.

It is not a megaphone, not a witching rod for poisons,
not a gun. It is not a moral compass.
It's just another world
the winter floods washed up from the creek,
                         and time comes
                              when a woman needs something heavy
                              to haul around.

Life Study Site: Bodega Natural Reserve

———————

Now I have a new husband, a spirit husband,
who walks out of the hills, the eastern hills,
with pine-pitch in his hair—

———————

Dune grass spread like a prairie rumor
from Bodega town to natural reserve
      (planted to keep homes unburied,
      rumored by a buzz in the breeze
      to be the New Prairie;
      sand gossips with roots about stability,
      while jittery San Andreas
      cuts right through the head);
reserve road bisects two translations
of "grassland": dune grass dominates on one side;
on the other, native ryegrass and yellow
bush lupine persist in feeding off the fog
and salty earth; this remnant native prairie was
heart-home to my husband.

———————

We asked what's driving the system
      of plants, although even the coastal prairie
              does not know all
         that occurs in a coastal prairie.

———————

He, the ecological researcher; I, his field hand:
      drop a Troxler down a vertically sunk
      PVC pipe, measure soil moisture as shifts
      in the tool's resonant frequency, irresistibly

jangled by water's dielectric constant.
Weed plots of experimental ryegrass plantings:
out with wild radish, out with native families
that ignored the study's boundaries.

The calm we gave each other can be measured over time
as an echo of the tick-ridden excitement
in our work preserving bits of native grassland.

———————————

Even kneeling in the sweet smell of torn roots,
I never narrowed my gaze
to exclude the fog. Still, I often failed
to stand and listen for the ocean,
just on the other side of hills hunkered
where there were once shifting dunes.

"All waters flow into it
                without filling it;
all water flows from it
                without draining it. . . ."

———————————

What kind of echo to the fog-
        horn is constructed
                in the cells of hardy dune grass?
        And in the rubbery fingers
                of iceplant gripping seaside cliffs?

———————————

This new husband is the man I married,
jolted out of temporal life,
broken into any of a thousand waves,
fragmented into wisps of pollen.
He walks out from under the lab
with water pipes for arms,
he walks up from seals, the bellow and bark of seals,
with granite crystal eyes.

                    (the shards of man's vertebrae
                    glitter five miles back
                    in the asphalt of the highway that led us here)
                                        —a sudden fog bank—

In one of the larger plots, I was counting culms
on a thriving dune grass bunch,
right arm encircling their sharp bulk,
left hand numbering off individual stalks.
One culm scratched my pupil.
I didn't notice until my eye started throbbing
a few hours later; all that morning, slopes of dune grass
shimmered at me like mirages.

        I gave my heart to the mule deer,
        their waggling tails and goofy ears,
        the way the herds could fizzle into mist
        as if each animal were only moisture's
        tawny muscles—
                I don't care who thinks my views are Bambified.
                I don't care if roadkill counters say
                the deer are doing fine.
                This is not about the phenomenon known as "deer."

I have a particular co-pathy
with this particular coastal prairie herd,
because we've been under the same saffron spell
of a hill of bush lupine in bloom,
                and they've watched me step through
                the drifting drapes of fog they've stepped through.
They're more aware of the effects
of drenched air on my wind-borne scent
than any human lover ever could be . . .

not to mention the ticks
we've shared. And dune grass simply
won't feed us at all.

—————————————

The eye seldom sees
what the mind does not anticipate—
shock is a tool to slice revelation
into the mind, into the grass, onto the once-
were dunes; my husband's accidental death
unveiled a world of unknowables.

Still, as I continue following the trail
of questions that we built together here,
                    I often forget (hill-blind,
                              were-dunes-blind,
                    vision striated by grasses)
the nearness of the pulsing sea.

Between Water and Song

Many ancient *americano*
    calendars agree—

this era is on its way out.
    One prophecy

says the next world
    will be water,

another says
    mundo floral.

Do we have time
    to argue the difference

between flower and water,
      water and song?

Why Can't We All Just Get Along?

Think of pink pickup trucks.

And picture dead Americans
Doing their Vietnam-era combat dying
In neat ethnic proportion.

All hail, the proportional dead!

Visualize nonperishable respect
Handed out in paper bags to neighbors.

A Dignity Pantry open 24 hours.

Then, I suppose, we could each
Have a friendly lick
Off the other's cone.

But this is your real Mother
On Public Assistance talking:

Is the salt in all these crackers
And canned goods
Not supposed to kill me?

Why can't I use these vouchers
For organic cheese and milk?
Why are the wealthy allowed to be healthier than me?

———————

Deep, cleansing breath everyone.
Oppression isn't rocket science.

It's easy enough
To ignore the torso
Of Evelyn Hernandez,
Afloat on the shore of the Bay
A year before Laci.
Her maternity shirt a billowing
Jelly-fish crown animated by waves,
Her case rejected from the rolls
Of *America's Most Wanted.*

SF Homicide tried spreading the word. . . .

I'm sorry to say, Evi, that without any
Lacey-white wedding photos to show,
Newsmakers thought no one would care much.

You were only 24, and being Salvadoran,
Maybe no one had shown you yet
How the gods of public opinion
Get fed around here.

The days of Good News are behind us;
Now a group of elites claiming expertise
On the whole Christ thing
Assures us He was way more uptight
About two men trying for wedded bliss
Than the brutal dismemberment of women
With names like "Hernandez."
  Sorry, señorita,
  The Bible's pretty clear on this one.

You don't need a PhD to see
This is a slap in the dead face
Of an entire chain of mothers,
Knotted and tangled together,
Circling down through history,

And coming to rest on the knifepoint
Of the present, as rosary beads circle down
To Christ's nailed feet.

While we're on the subject
Of murdered muchachas,
Could someone please
Ask the slaughtered
Daughters of Juárez
Not to shriek so loudly
At night? They're bothering
Some nice people in Texas.
Would they mind not being so *political*
All the time?

    (Say the p-word as though invoking the name
    of a hated vegetable, e.g.,

        "Could you not be so *lima bean* all the time!")

Everyone knows that only a few Texans,
Only a few Americans,
Get to be political.
And then, only on TV.

I'm not an angry person, really.
I've never yelled at the snow for
Melting,
Or cursed a grasshopper
For disappearing into the weeds
When I wanted to catch it.

A river killed a man I loved,
And I love that river still.

Rough treatment from the Great Beyond?
I've come to expect it.

But someone—who?
The Son of Man?—
Told me I could expect better
From the hands
Of humans.

In all fondness for the grasshoppers, I say
My neighbors and I
Are no better than insects.

———————

May the peace of legally recognized newlyweds
Be with us all,

And may Evelyn's broken breath,
As recorded in the Bay waves,
Fill our ears until we're deaf
To the Call for Complacency.

Has it been whispered all along?

She lifted death from Poudre River,
curled it up in her arms—no
body (she arrived too late), but death
remained like flood debris,
so she carried it until the weight became
fiber in the bolls of her shoulders;

you know the facts—
her lover guiding a raft of tourists
down Pineview Falls,
the raft flipping, and the rescue
of all the customers by other boaters,
the way he waved off the safety rope,
floated conscious for a quarter mile,
stood up at last in the shallows
and took a few steps before collapsing
from a broken neck—

how his friend called to tell her,
and she screamed *stop joking*—how
she dreamed of him that night,
walking naked towards her,
muscles twisting like water
in his lean form.

A tree knows the whole story—
manzanita, red and gray wood
intertwined, alive and dead,
knows she made his death

a skeletal ladder, knows death rode
her every twist and growing knot
while she rose toward the reeling
of the sky—

Maybe death is the wildest movement of all,
and in this arid range we inhabit
there is moisture to be found at the boundary
between the two woods.

Maybe you can follow the orange-waisted ants
into the tiny space left
between living and dead;
maybe what looks like a line of demarcation
is actually an alcove,
a feast of hidden droplets—

NOTES

Remedio
Recent research points to the strong possibility that the reintroduction of wolves
into Yellowstone National Park may be causing the increased vigor of streamside
vegetation communities; these communities had previously been overbrowsed to
the point of local near-extinction by big ungulate prey species. See http://www
.cof.orst.edu/wolves/ and http://nature.berkeley.edu/~cwilmers/.

In the Early Months of Snowmelt, 1997
Lines 21–22 come from a thirteenth-century Chinese landscape painting, by way
of Gary Snyder's *Mountains and Rivers Without End* (Washington, DC: Coun-
terpoint, 1996).

In Biruté's Camp
In her book *Reflections of Eden: My Years with the Orangutans of Borneo* (Bos-
ton: Little, Brown, 1995), Biruté Galdikas, a prominent researcher of orangutan
ecology, documents the rape of one of her camp assistants by a male ex-captive
orangutan named Gundul.

Art of Combat
Based on a black-and-white silver print in the *Cosmic Pugilist* series by Francisco
Dominguez.

Learning to Speak: Carolina
This poem references a traditional Cherokee account of the origin of stars in the
constellation some call Pleiades, which demonstrates the familial relationship
between the stars, longleaf pines, and humans.

Collections of Nearly Unlovable Spaces
Line 10, thanks to Tony Hoagland.

Tonacacihuatl
See *Snake Poems,* Francisco X. Alarcón (San Francisco: Chronicle Books, 1992).

American Adhaan
The Adhaan is the set of phrases spoken during the Muslim call to prayer.

Recipe for When You're Tired . . .
Adapted from *The Natural World of the California Indians,* Robert F. Heizer and Albert B. Elsasser (Berkeley: University of California Press, 1981).

Llorona's Guide to Baptism
In various Mexican and Chicano stories, La Llorona is a figure who can be heard weeping near water. In some accounts, she weeps because her children have drowned, in others she weeps because she herself has killed them.

Life Study Site: Bodega Natural Reserve
This poem began as I accompanied ecologists Eric Knapp and Kevin Rice in their fieldwork at Bodega Natural Reserve. The speaking persona was, in part, inspired by the life of the great American conservationist Margaret Murie.

Between Water and Song
¡Viva el floricanto!

Has it been whispered all along?
See "Out of the Cradle, Endlessly Rocking," by Walt Whitman.

ACKNOWLEDGMENTS

Thank you to the editors at the following journals, in which some of these poems have appeared: *Art/Life, Ecological Restoration, ISLE, Organization & Environment, Perihelion, Tiger's Eye,* and *Tule Review.*

Seven of these poems were originally published in the chapbook *Base Pairs* (Swan Scythe Press, 2001). Thanks are due to Steve Culberson and Sandra McPherson for editing and publishing this volume.

The following anthologies include poems published here; I am grateful to these editors and publishers for their dedication to new literature. *Comeback Wolves: Western Writers Welcome the Wolf Home,* SueEllen Campbell, Gregory McNamee, Gary Wockner, editors (Johnson Books, 2005); *Hunger Enough: Living Spiritually in a Consumer Society,* Nita Penfold, editor (Pudding House Publications, 2004); *Mark My Words: Five Emerging Poets,* Francisco Aragón, editor (Momotombo Press, 2001); *Sisters of the Earth: Women's Prose and Poetry About Nature* (2nd edition), Lorraine Anderson, editor (Vintage Books, 2003); and *Under the Fifth Sun: Latino Literature from California,* Rick Heide, editor (Heyday Books, 2002).

For friendship, guidance, collaboration, and inspiration I thank Francisco X. Alarcón, Francisco Aragón, Nancy Arora, Steven Cordova, Phebe Davidson, Holly Dolan, Diana García, Laurie Glover, Patti Hartmann, Dan Leroy, Sandra McPherson, Yosefa Raz, David Robertson, Gary Snyder, y ellas de la Tierra Chicana.

For invaluable collegial and financial support during the years these poems were written, I offer gratitude to all involved with CLICA, Hedgebrook writers' retreat, the Putah-Cache Bioregion Project, and the Saint Mary's College Department of English and Center for Women's InterCultural Leadership. Lastly, and most essentially, I extend my deepest gratitude to my family.

ABOUT THE AUTHOR

María Meléndez has sold athletic shoes, canvassed for political organizations, and worked as a wildlife biology field assistant, among many other jobs. While completing graduate studies in creative writing at the University of California, Davis, she served as an Area Coordinator for California Poets in the Schools. In 2000, she was awarded an Artists-in-Communities grant from the California Arts Council to support her work as writer-in-residence at the UC Davis Arboretum, where she taught environmental poetry workshops for the public. She is currently Assistant Professor of English at Saint Mary's College in Notre Dame, Indiana, where she teaches creative writing and multiethnic literatures and directs the Writing Proficiency Program. She has authored one chapbook of poetry, *Base Pairs,* and edited two anthologies, *Nest of Freedom* and *Moon Won't Leave Me Alone.* She also serves as Associate Editor for Momotombo Press, and her poetry, articles, and short fiction appear in a number of magazines, such as *Puerto del Sol* and *International Quarterly.*

10/15 n/c
LAD 07/14

**Indianapolis
Marion County
Public Library**

Renew by Phone
269-5222

Renew on the Web
www.imcpl.org

For General Library Information
please call 269-1700